How CIOs Can Take Their Career To The Next Level

How CIOs Can Work With The Entire Company In Order To Be Successful

"Practical, proven techniques that will help you to make your CIO career long and successful"

Dr. Jim Anderson

Published by

Blue Elephant Consulting

Tampa, Florida

Printed in the United States of America

Library of Congress Control Number: 2017934571

ISBN-13: 978-1543248395
ISBN-10: 154324839X

Warning – Disclaimer

Recent Books By The Author

Product Management

- Manage Your Customers, Manage Your Product: Techniques For Product Managers To Better Understand What Their Customers Really Want

- Managing Your Product Manager Career: How Product Managers Can Find And Succeed In The Right Job

Public Speaking

- How To Get Ready To Give The Perfect Speech: What Tools To Use To Create Your Next Speech So That Your Message Will Be Remembered Forever!

- Creating Speeches That Work: How To Create A Speech That Will Make Your Message Be Remembered Forever!

CIO Skills

- How CIOs Can Bring Business And IT Together: How CIOs Can Use Their Technical Skills To Help Their Company Solve Real-World Business Problems

- New IT Technology Issues Facing CIOs: How CIOs Can Stay On Top Of The Changes In The Technology That

Powers The Company

IT Manager Skills

- How IT Managers Can Use New Technology To Meet Today's IT Challenges: Technologies That IT Managers Can Use In Order to Make Their Teams More Productive

- How To Build High Performance IT Teams: Tips And Techniques That IT Managers Can Use In Order To Develop Productive Teams

Negotiating

- The Art Of Packaging A Negotiation: How To Develop The Skill Of Assembling Potential Trades In Order To Get The Best Possible Outcome

- Getting What You Want In A Negotiation By Learning How To Signal: How To Develop The Skill Of Effective Signaling In A Negotiation In Order To Get The Best Possible Outcome

Miscellaneous

- How To Heal A Broken Leg – Fast!: Understanding how to deal with a broken leg in order to start walking again quickly

- How Software Defined Networking (SDN) Is Going To Change Your World Forever: The Revolution In Network Design And How It Affects

- **Note**: See a complete list of books by Dr. Jim Anderson at the back of this book.

Acknowledgements

Any book like this one is the result of years of real-world work experience. In my over 25 years of working for 7 different firms, I have met countless fantastic people and I've been mentored by some truly exceptional ones. Although I've probably forgotten some of the people who made me the person that I am today, here is my attempt to finally give them the recognition that they so truly deserve:

- Thomas P. Anderson
- Art Puett
- Bobbi Marshall
- Bob Boggs

Dr. Jim Anderson

This book is dedicated to my wife Lori. None of this would have been possible without her love and support.

Thanks for the best years of my life (so far)...!

Speaking.   Negotiating.   Managing.   Marketing.

Table Of Contents

You Are Responsible For Taking Your Career To The Next Level

It's only after you become a CIO that you truly start to understand all of the things that you don't know. Your technical skills are probably what got you this job, but they are not going to be enough to allow you to keep it. You are going to have to decide if it's going to take getting an MBA to allow you to get a seat at the table with the company's other decision makers.

You want to become more than just a CIO, you want to become a high potential CIO who is known for going places. In order for this to happen, you are going to have to take action. You are going to have to find ways to make yourself valuable to your company.

Ultimately it all comes down to just exactly how much responsibility you are going to be willing to accept. The more that you are willing to take on, the more valuable you will become to the company. However, you need to be very careful and not go too far – the authority granted to you as CIO can be abused and then you may find yourself in a very difficult place.

The CIO job that you have today may not be your last job. If you are going to make a move to another CIO job, then you are going to want to make sure that you do it correctly. The last thing that you would want to do would be to make the wrong move.

In order to make the most of the CIO position, you need to be listened to by your company. This means that you need to be part of the right type of reporting structure. Not every industry gets this right; however, right now the power industry is starting to realize the importance of the CIO and it's a good place for a CIO to be.

To fully develop your CIO career is going to take a great deal of personal energy. This means that you are going to have to make sure that you have what it will take to be successful. No, you won't always be successful, but that's ok. Even the best of us stumble occasionally, but then we get right back up.

For more information on what it takes to be a successful CIO, check out my blog, The Accidental Successful CIO, at:

www.TheAccidentalSuccessfulCIO.com

Good luck!

- Dr. Jim Anderson

About The Author

I must confess that I never set out to be a CIO. When I went to school, I studied Computer Science and thought that I'd get a nice job programming and that would be that. Well, at least part of that plan worked out!

My first job was working for Boeing on their F/A-18 fighter jet program. I spent my days programming fighter jet software in assembly language and I loved it. The U.S. government decided to save some money and went looking for other countries to sell this plane to. This put me into an unfamiliar role: I started to meet with foreign military officials and I ended up having to manage groups of engineers who were working on international projects.

Time moved on and so did I. I found myself working for Siemens, the big German telecommunications company. They were making phone switches and selling them to the seven U.S. phone companies. The problem was that the switches were too complicated. Customers couldn't tell the difference between one complicated phone switch from another complicated phone switch. Once again I found myself working with the sales and marketing teams to find ways to make the great technology that the engineers had developed understandable to both internal and external customers.

I've spent over 25 years working as an senior IT professional for both big companies and startups. This has given me an opportunity to learn what it takes to manage and IT department in ways that allow it to maximize its output while becoming a valuable part of the overall company.

I now live in Tampa Florida where I spend my time managing my consulting business, Blue Elephant Consulting, teaching college courses at the University of South Florida, and traveling to work with companies like yours to share the knowledge that I have about how to create and manage successful IT departments.

I'm always available to answer questions and I can be reached at:

Dr. Jim Anderson
Blue Elephant Consulting
Email: jim@BlueElephantConsulting.com
Facebook: http://goo.gl/1TVoK
Web: http://www.BlueElephantConsulting.com/

"Unforgettable communication skills that will set your ideas free..."

Create IT Departments That Are Productive And A Valuable Asset To The Rest Of The Company !

Dr. Jim Anderson is available to provide training and coaching on the topics that are the most important to people who have to manage IT departments: how can I build a productive IT department (and keep it together) while at the same time providing the rest of the company with the IT services that they need?

Dr. Anderson believes that in order to both learn and remember what he says, speakers need to laugh. Each one of his speeches is full of fun and humor so that what he says "sticks" with everyone.

Dr. Anderson's CIO Skills Training Includes:

1. How to identify and attract the right type of IT workers to your IT department.
2. How to build relationships with the company's senior management in order to get the support that you need?
3. How to stay on top of changing technology and security issues so that you never get surprised?

Dr. Jim Anderson works with over 100 customers per year. To invite Dr. Anderson to work with you, contact him at:

Phone: 813-418-6970 or
Email: jim@BlueElephantConsulting.com

12

13

Chapter 1

CIO's With No Time Find An Alternative To An MBA

Chapter 1: CIO's With No Time Find An Alternative To An MBA

As CIO wanna-be's who live in troubling times we are always trying to do two things: hold on to our jobs and be more successful. One of the best ways to do both of these, or so we have been told, is to **go out and get an MBA**. Well that's all great and fine if you've got four or five years to burn, don't need to do anything else at night, oh and have a big chunk of cash sitting around that you had no other plans for. Maybe it's time to look for a better way to accomplish what we're trying to do...

Say Hello To The Alternative To The MBA

Before you decide to either quit your IT job and go back to school in order to get an MBA (really, really expensive) or start going to night school to get an MBA (just really expensive), maybe you should take a moment and **consider all of your options**. Maybe what you really want is a specialized Master's degree.

Yeah, yeah – I know what you are thinking. We've all been drinking the "get an MBA" Kool-Aid for so long that it's hard to imagine doing anything else. However, depending on what you want to do with your life, **this might actually be a better solution for you**.

If having spent time being on the IT side of the company has gotten you interested in what goes on over on the business side, then getting an advanced business degree of some sort is probably a good idea. However, one of the things that keeps us from doing this is often **the time involved to get the degree**.

The Appeal Of Specializing

Business schools and online universities are starting to get the message. They are beginning to offer more and more specialized business programs that are only 12 months long. In the 2008-2009 school year **there were 645 programs offered**. This is up from the 614 programs that had been offered just two years earlier.

What these types of degrees offer are parts of the typical MBA curriculum, but they are often more technical in nature and generally **spend less time on general management skills**.

Here in lies the rub: these types of specialty business degrees are not designed to get you promoted to eventually become the CEO. Rather what they are designed to do is to sharpen your business skills in a narrow area and **make you more valuable to the company in your current job**. Since we're interested in becoming the CIO, not the CEO, this might be just what we're looking for.

This type of continuing education especially appeals to **new IT professionals**: those who don't have the five years of work experience that most MBA programs require for entrance. No matter if this is your case, or if you've just found some part of the company's business side that you are really drawn to, a narrowly focused master's degree might be just the ticket for you.

What To Do With Your New Degree

Ok, so let's say that you bite the bullet and run off and skip the MBA and instead get a very focused master's degree in marketing, finance, or some other business discipline. **What then?**

It turns out that taking this path, might feel like the right thing for you to do, but as they like to say on TV, **your results may vary**. Since specialty master's degrees are not as well-known as MBA's you're going to have to deal with some lack of recognition issues.

Although it may change in the future, right now **MBA students still seem to get the best deal** when it comes to getting the economic benefits from going through the effort of getting an advanced degree. The people who design the GMAT test that everyone takes to get admitted to graduate programs are reporting that MBA students are saying that they get a 73% increase in salary after graduating while students with specialty master's degrees are only reporting a 26% increase.

What All Of This Means For You

In the end **the decision rests with you**. We all know that continuing our education is an important thing for every up-and-coming almost CIO to do. Going back to school almost seems like a no-brainer until you realize that you need to spend some time thinking about just what you want to get out of doing so.

A specialty master's degree offers IT professionals who have been working for less than five years or who found one particular part of the job most interesting with a new option. By investing 12 months of study, they can walk away with both another degree as well as **a deep understanding** of one area of business.

The value of taking this educational route will really depend on the career that you want for yourself. If you are comfortable working inside of the business instead of running it, then a specialty master's degree **might be the right way to go for you!**

Chapter 2

How CIOs Can Get What They Don't Have (But Really Need)

Chapter 2: How CIOs Can Get What They Don't Have (But Really Need)

Not being invited to sit at the company's **strategy table** is a problem that has plagued CIOs since the position was invented. Instead of just talking about the problem, it's high time we did something to turn things around. But what should we do?

Skill Building

The reason that CIOs aren't being asked to contribute in a significant way to the types of decisions that go into running the company as a whole is because the rest of the senior management team **doesn't believe that the CIO has the skills that are needed** to contribute to this process in a meaningful way. Unfortunately they are correct more often than not.

Sure, your average CIO has the technical skill set that got him / her into the position that they now hold; however, that's not enough to get them invited to participate in **running the company** in a meaningful way. What they are viewed as missing are critical skills such as finance, marketing, R&D, etc.

Coming Up With A Plan

In an ideal world, a newly minted CIO would be able to sign up for a **specialized course (or set of courses)** that would teach the very skills that he / she is missing. We're not talking about college courses here, these would have to be very specialized.

What the CIO would want to (really have to) learn is exactly what the role of IT needs to be in order to **help each of the other parts of the company**. The focus wouldn't be on technology, but rather it would be on just exactly how IT could be used to maximize the performance of each of the pieces that make up the company. An emphasis on how things are in the real-world instead of in dry textbooks would also be a key to successful leaning.

How To Do This In The Real World

Sadly, I don't think that such a set of courses currently exists. Don't give up hope, it just means that when you become CIO you're going to have to take a different path. Your home-brew educational program is going to have to consist of **three main steps**:

Every company has a set of educational programs that they offer. Generally these are designed to teach workers about what the company does and just exactly how it does it. These courses are often taught by other workers who have years of experience. CIOs need to sign up and show up for these classes – the information that they'll cover is like gold to a CIO.

Eat Lunch With Different People Every Day: CIOs need to introduce themselves to as many managers throughout the company as possible. This is how they are going to learn how the different departments work and what challenges they are facing. This isn't exactly a classroom, but rather it's like getting a complete education one conversation at a time.

Forget About Technology: While a CIO is learning about the different parts that make up the company and just exactly what they do, issues of technology need to be left behind. Once an understanding of how the company runs has been achieved, then the technology discussions can start, but while the learning is going on the CIO needs to shut up and fit in.

What All Of This Means For You

CIOs don't know what they don't know. This is what is keeping them from being invited by the rest of a company's senior management to participate in the business of plotting out the company's strategic direction. CIO's need to get the training that will provide them with the skills that they are missing.

Although specialized training would be the best way to get this information, CIOs are going to have to **build their own training program**. This will include signing up for internal company courses, talking with managers from other departments, and leaving technology behind for a while.

In the end, a CIO is the one person in the company who is best positioned to **find ways to use technology to solve the problems that the company is facing**. However, before they can do that, they've got to go back to school and do some more learning...

Chapter 3

---

5 Ways For CIOs To Become (Much) More Important

Chapter 3: 5 Ways For CIOs To Become (Much) More Important

Once you become the CIO you'd think that you've have it made. Now that you are living at the top of the IT pyramid, life should be grand – the long, hard struggle to reach this position is now over. Actually, **the job is just beginning**. What you need to do now is to find ways to make sure that the CIO becomes a (more) important part of your company's success. Here are some suggestions for how you can make this happen.

It's All About The Cloud

Just as much as the next guy, I hate to jump on the "what's trendy in IT" bandwagon; however, it's really starting to look as though this cloud computing thing is **here to stay**. Looks like you're going to have to come up with ways to work it into your IT department's strategy.

The key thing for you to do is to understand why it's so important. Cloud computing offers the CIO the ability to **kill two birds with one stone**: you have the ability to reduce your IT costs while at the same time allowing the company to expand its IT footprint. Opportunities like this don't come along often enough and so you had better jump on it while it's available to you.

Flipping the 80/20 Rule

When you become the CIO, one of the first things that you're going to discover is **just how little money you have to spend**. Oh, your IT budget might be huge and it may be growing larger every year, but the size of the funds that are actually available to you to spend on new projects and new initiatives is probably quite small by comparison.

So where's all the money going? In a nutshell, most of your IT budget is going to be spent just keeping the lights on – maintenance on all of those embedded applications that run the company today. This has got to change.

As CIO you are going to have to get your sharp budget knife out and **start making cuts**. Any IT support functions that don't contribute to moving the company forward need to be moved from the inside to the outside. Free up more IT budget for transformation projects and everyone will view you as the best CIO ever.

Growing The Business / Growing The Customer

Although you don't often hear about the CIO being talked about in the same sentence that **revenue growth** is mentioned, this is what you need to make happen. The reason the business exists is to generate more money, the IT department has to play a role in this or it becomes unnecessary.

Make sure that you don't do what some CIOs have done and go out and **start selling your own products**. The role of IT is to support what the company does. IT's contribution to the company's top line revenue should be a result of how it helps other departments become more efficient.

Following Business Processes From End-To-End

The role of CIO is unique in the company: you actually have **very few restrictions on what you are permitted to do**. This is a fantastic gift that you need to take advantage of.

With the ability to follow a process from where it starts in the company to where it ends, a CIO can **find things that nobody else can**: waste, miscommunications, opportunities for automation, etc.

Introducing Business Intelligence

Most businesses do a good job of **collecting lots of data** on how the business is running. Very few businesses do a good job of using the data that they've collected.

The CIO has an opportunity to implement **business intelligence solutions** that can provide the rest of the company with new insights. This type of value add is exactly what the rest of the company needs their CIO to do for them.

What All Of This Means For You

When you become CIO, **the real work is just starting**. You are going to have to be constantly looking for ways to add value to the rest of the company.

There are many ways for you to do this. Some rely on technology such as how best to use cloud computing or implementing business intelligence solutions. However, more of them have to do with the business side of IT: maximizing your IT budget and improving the company's end-to-end business processes.

CIOs that focus on improving the company's revenues **will be spending their time wisely**. By doing so, they'll create an opportunity to hang around and do even greater things in the future...

Chapter 4

What It Takes To Become A
High Potential CIO

Chapter 4: What It Takes To Become A High Potential CIO

What is it going to take to make your CIO career a success? Sure, you can deliver IT value and get your projects done on time, but will that be enough? The answer is no. For you to be seen as a successful CIO you are going to have to be seen as **a "high potential" CIO** – one who is going to go places beyond your current assignment. Clearly you need to know what it's going to take to get others to consider you to be high potential...

The Intangibles

The reason that many CIOs get stuck in their current job with the current responsibilities is because others don't believe that they have **"what it takes"** to handle other responsibilities. The things that it will take for you to be viewed as being a high potential are intangible (can't really be expressed in words) and generally can't be written down on job descriptions or yearly evaluations.

The good news is that Dr. Douglas Ready and a team of researchers have been looking into what it takes for an IT worker to move from regular to high potential workers. They've uncovered **four factors** that can transform you from every day to high potential in the eyes of others.

Drive Time

Do you have what it takes to succeed? Can others tell that you have this drive? Just being good isn't enough for you – **you have to want to be great** and it needs to show.

The key here is that others need to be able to determine that you are willing to **make the extra effort to succeed**. This means that they are going to have to be able to see you make sacrifices in order to advance in your career. Everyone has to know that your personal life comes second when it comes to your job.

The Ability To Learn / Do

High potential CIOs are **always learning new things**. However, this isn't enough. Just because you are willing to constantly be learning new things doesn't make you a high potential IT worker.

Instead, you need to show others that you have the ability to not only learn new things, but to also take what you've learned and **apply it to what is happening right now**. The use of new ideas to make IT more productive for the company is what is going to set you apart from everyone else.

Become A Risk Taker

Despite all of us understanding that IT is all about change, it can be too easy for CIOs **to get comfortable in their jobs**. When this happens, they lose the desire to take new risks and they are no longer viewed by others as being high potential CIOs.

What we need to do is to be willing to **take on new ways to make the company more productive**. Sometimes this involves starting a risky new project, or developing a new set of IT skills that will require us to leave what we already know behind.

Develop Your "Spidy Sense"

The comic book hero Spiderman has what he calls his **"spidy sense"** which tingles when there is danger approaching. High potential CIOs need to develop their own version of this type of sensing that allows them to detect when a danger to their careers is approaching.

Career dangers can include such things as projects that are doomed to fail from the start, or avoiding providing feedback to senior managers that could help the company do better. High potential CIOs have a highly developed sense that allows them to know **when to push forward and when to pull back**.

What All Of This Means For You

Just being a CIO is not enough. In fact, just being a good CIO is not enough either. What you want to be is **a high-potential CIO**. This will open doors to new opportunities at the firm that you are working for and at other firms also.

In order to start to be seen as being "high potential", you are going to have to **start doing several things**. These include showing a keen sense of drive to succeed, the ability to both learn new things and then apply what you've learned, take proper risks, and sense when an opportunity is either a good thing or a bad thing for your career.

The good news is that **any CIO can become a high potential CIO**. Simply by adopting these traits you can quickly move from being seen as simply a good CIO to being seen as a high potential CIO.

Chapter 5

The "R" Word And What It Means To CIOs

Chapter 5: The "R" Word And What It Means To CIOs

CIOs have a tough job and we all know it. However, because it is so tough, it can be easy to lose sight of **what is really important**. As we look for ways to cut costs, boost innovation, retain key employees and simply make IT more relevant to the rest of the company, our vision can start to drift downwards towards the daily tasks and short term goals. This is when we can forget what our real job is – to show the rest of the company what responsibility really is.

The Things That Are Important

Dr. C.K. Prahalad spent time thinking about what is really important. I believe that he's come up with a great set of things that **CIOs need to be focusing on** and they all have to do with responsibility.

CIO's need to realize that in order to move the IT department and the company forward, **they can't always play by the rules**. The rules are what got everyone to where they are today. In order to get to where you need to be in the future, you can't keep doing the same things.

You are going to need to have **the courage to try new things**. To go places where people have not gone before. When you do this, others are going to tell you that you are breaking the rules, doing things that shouldn't be done. You will have to have the courage and fortitude to stay the course in order to map out these uncharted lands.

You will need to realize that you truly don't know it all. In fact, you probably don't know most of what you are going to have to know going forward. This means that **you are going to have to always be learning**. The key here is to be able to admit that you don't know it all and that you need to find others who will be willing to teach you what you still need to learn.

Being a CIO is not a point in time, but rather a journey. You have to take **the long-term perspective** in everything that you do. During your career you will have some amazing successes and some spectacular failures. You are going to need to learn how to be modest when you have done good and you are going to have to find ways to keep going on when things don't go your way.

The Role That Other People Play

Being a CIO is very much like being a farmer. It's not all about the farm, but rather about what you raise on the farm that will determine how much of a success you will eventually be. CIOs don't grow crops, but we do grow people. One of your most important jobs is **to develop the next generation of IT leaders**.

Not everyone will have your skills or talents. As CIO you need to realize this and you need to find ways to work with them. It is all too easy to discard or ignore those who don't measure up to what we think everyone should be. However, the world doesn't always look the way that we think that it should and **we are the ones who need to change** in order to make it a better place, not everyone else.

Although we don't talk about it enough, loyalty is one of the most important things that we can bring to the role of CIO. We want our team to be loyal to us, but we need to **show them what that means** by being loyal to them and to those around us.

CIOs need to be willing to **take responsibility** for the ways that things turn out. Ultimately it is our IT department that we are running and everything that happens in it is our responsibility.

We can't just accept the praise for the things that go well and run from the blame for the things that don't turn out how we had hoped. We are all in this together.

What All Of This Means For You

To become a CIO is truly an honor – the company has selected you **to lead the IT department**. Yes, there are great things expected of you, but at the same time there are unspoken expectations also.

You are to show the rest of the company **just what responsibility really means**. Others can hide or avoid doing what has been asked of them, you don't have such luxuries. You stand alone in the company's spotlight and you are going to have to deliver.

The good news is that you wouldn't have been given the job if others didn't think that you could do it. There's no question that you've got the technical skills to be CIO. It's all of the other things, **the "soft skills"** that will tax you on a daily basis. As long as you realize that it's your job to show the rest of the company what responsibility really means, then you'll end up doing just fine.

Chapter 6

Advice To CIOs: Don't Do What I Did...

Chapter 6: Advice To CIOs: Don't Do What I Did...

How long until you end up in jail? They say that power corrupts and that absolute power corrupts absolutely, so it sure seems as though just about **every CIO will eventually become corrupted**. How far along that path are you? Would it help if you had a chance to talk to someone who had already screwed up – do you think that maybe what they'd have to say might cause you to sit up, take notice, and stop doing bad things and start doing the right things?

Say Hello To Aaron Beam

Aaron Beam was the CFO of HealthSouth, a very large company that provides rehabilitation services. Aaron worked as their CFO during a period of **incredible growth**.

HealthSouth had grown to become a Fortune 500 company by 1994. At the time they had over 40,000 employees in all 50 states and in Alabama alone they were the largest company. Their **annual growth numbers** were in the range of 20% – 30% which is fantastic for any company.

The company's CEO, Richard Scrushy was not a nice guy. Former employees report that he was a very hard man to say "no" to. His personal style was that **he would become very angry over even the smallest things**. His employees were actually afraid to be in the same room with him when he blew his top.

How Did Things Go So Very Wrong?

As any CIO can tell you, working for a young company that is growing like a weed is a great place to be. In Aaron Beam's case, however, **it quickly went all wrong**.

As with all such ethical lapses, **it started out innocently enough**. HealthSouth could not keep up with its furious growth rate. This was going to cause a problem because if investors saw its growth rate start to slow down, the value of HealthSouth's stock would start to decrease.

In order to prevent this from happening, Beam started to decrease the amount of money the company set aside to cover bad debts. He also started to **change the estimated value of the companies that they were buying** because they could then apply those estimates to the company's earnings as they went forward.

These actions were shady, but not out and out illegal. **Then Beam did a very bad thing**. The finance team finally reached a point where changing estimates would no longer produce the kind of numbers that they needed to show solid growth. Something else needed to be done.

What they ended up doing was fraudulently entering a lot of small entries into their books that they hoped would slip by the auditors. The first time that they did this was in 1996 and the company **kept on doing it** through 2002.

As is always the case, **the fraud was eventually found out**. Beam ended up spending three months in a minimum–security prison. He's had to give up his earnings in order to pay fines and his legal bills. He now operates a lawn mowing business and speaks on ethics at universities.

The lesson here for CIOs is that **the temptation to do wrong is always out there**. It never shows up as a clear "right / wrong" type of decision. Instead, it starts out as a small ethical decision and if you choose the wrong path, you'll end up making many more decisions that you'll eventually come to regret.

What All Of This Means For You

CIOs wield a great deal of power and it can be easy to start to think that **we don't have to play by the same rules as everyone else**. Nothing could be farther from the truth.

Aaron Beam was the CFO for HealthSouth when he faced **an ethical dilemma**: should he commit financial fraud to keep the company growing, or should he tell the truth and perhaps cause serious harm to the company. He chose to commit the fraud and ended up spending time in jail for doing so.

The real world that CIOs live in is not made up of nice black and white decisions. **There's a lot of gray out there**. CIOs need to spend the time taking ethical training and thinking about different situations that they may find themselves in. Only by doing this will they be ready to make the right decision when the day comes that they'll be tempted to make the wrong decision.

Chapter 7

Only A CIO Could Screw Up A Job Change!

Chapter 7: Only A CIO Could Screw Up A Job Change!

The global economy is roaring back again and it sure seems like everyone is starting to take stock of their job and decide if they want to stay where they are or **move on to greener pastures**. CIOs are no exception. Perhaps you've grown as far as you can or perhaps you feel that you've done everything that you're going to be allowed to do where you are at. If you are thinking about moving on, you had better be careful that you don't screw up your job change...

Failing To Do Enough Research On Where You Are Going

Considering the fact that doing research, collecting data, and then making the best possible decision is such **a key part of the job of being a CIO**, you'd think that we'd all do this well when it comes to looking for our next job. Well, guess again.

The folks who know such things, search consultants, say that CIOs are dropping the ball in several areas. The first is that they don't do a good job of **sizing up the market for their skills**. What this means is that CIOs don't have valid assumptions for how long it's going to take to find their next job.

Next, CIOs somewhat surprisingly don't do a good job of checking out the financial health of the company that they are thinking about jumping to. Sure they may check out the technology, but not **the bottom line situation**.

Additionally, the culture of the new company is **rarely considered**. If a CIO is coming in from a free-wheeling Silicon Valley company and is considering going to work for a 100-year old insurance firm, culture becomes a big deal.

Finally, all too often CIOs assume that they are getting what's being advertised – that **the job title matches the job**. Just because the new company calls the job "CIO" does not mean that you'll have the same level of control that you had in your old job.

Going When They Show You The Money

Hey, I like money, you like money. However, as hard as it is for both of us to understand, you can't leave one job and go to another just because the new job pays more. **This is a sure recipe for disaster**.

When CIOs were asked to rank what they were looking for in a new job, pay came in at the fourth or fifth place on the list. However, all too often CIOs bump this factor up to first place **when it comes time to make a decision** — bad move.

Deciding To Go "From" Rather Than "To"

Just like everyone else out there, CIOs can become **dissatisfied with their jobs**. When this happens, they can start to make poor career decisions.

When a CIO decides to switch jobs, it should be **a carefully planned career move**. However, if they are really upset with their current position, then all too often it becomes just a desperate jump to the nearest lifeboat. Since this often happens with little or no serious research into the firm that the CIO is fleeing to, these new positions rarely last for long.

As a CIO bounces from firm to firm, you can quickly develop a reputation as **a job hopper** and it will become that much harder to get your next job. No matter how bad your current job is, take the time to plan out what your next career step should be before you do anything.

What All Of This Means For You

CIOs are like everyone else: when the opportunity to move to a new job comes along, they can decide to make the jump for all of the wrong reasons. If you are aware of the most common mistakes that other CIOs have made, then you'll have a chance to avoid them.

The mistakes that CIOs make are easily avoidable. The most common mistakes include not doing enough research on the company that they'll be joining, being seduced by an offer of more money, and focusing on leaving the firm where they are and not taking a careful look at just exactly where they'll be going.

Ultimately, being aware of the most common mistakes that CIOs make is the first step in avoiding them. You can switch jobs smoothly and end up in a better place, just make sure that you're switching for all the right reasons!

Chapter 8

Now What? When CIOs Make The Wrong Job Move...

Chapter 8: Now What? When CIOs Make The Wrong Job Move...

Sure you did all of the research, you talked with all of the right people, shucks you even followed up on every Google link that you could find on the company that you were thinking about going to work for before making the jump. However, now that you've made the jump you are finding out that perhaps **you've made a mistake**. Now what do you do?

How Did This Happen?

CIOs are supposed to be smart people, how come we can end up making mistakes when it comes time to switch jobs? The good news is that we are smart; however, what can happen is that we can find ourselves under a great deal of pressure and this can **adversely affect how we make decisions**.

One such type of pressure is mental pressure – **how do we see ourselves**? When we are considering making a job change, we tend to make up our minds about how we think the next job is going to be and then we only pay attention to the information that we encounter that confirms this view. Researchers call this thinking "confirmation bias".

In order to counter this kind of thinking we need to be constantly asking ourselves one question: **what happens if I am wrong?** Only by doing this will you be able to make yourself aware of information that might not fit the way that you want the world to be.

Another type of pressure you need to deal with when you are considering changing jobs is social pressure. This is most often evident when you have become so unhappy with your current job that **you'd almost rather be anywhere else**.

Far too often these types of situations could be dealt with if you would only find the courage to sit down and **talk things over with someone at your current company**. However, all too often we are so resistant to having this kind of discussion that we're willing to leave the firm and run to a new job.

Finally, the ever present specter of time pressure is always a factor when it comes to considering moving to a new job. When we don't feel that we have very much time to make a decision, what happens is that **we end up hastily making a bad decision**.

The lack of time forces us to **focus on the short-term gains** that we'll make by switching jobs. What happens is that we forget to take a look at the long-term impacts of making the switch. A good way of countering this tendency is to ask yourself questions such as "if the salaries & benefits were the same, would I make the job switch?"

What Do You Do Now?

Despite having taken the time to carefully consider all of the issues and to try to counter the pressures that will be driving your decision, sometimes we still end up making poor job change choices. The question then comes up: **what should we do now?**

The experts all agree on the answer to this one. You need to **cut your losses** and move on once again. However, this time around you need to do a better job. Don't just flee a bad job and jump yet again into another poor position. Take the time to understand why you made a bad job change decision and make sure that you don't repeat this mistake.

Ultimately the best way to protect yourself from making another bad career decision is to **become more self-aware**. You want to be able to understand your strengths and weaknesses so that you can evaluate your next job opportunity in a way that will reveal if it is really the right career move for you.

What All Of This Means For You

Despite our best efforts, sometimes we make mistakes when we are **switching jobs**. There can be a number of different reasons that we make this kind of mistake but more often than not they all come back to the different types of pressures that we are under: mental, social, or time.

If you find yourself having made the wrong choice in switching jobs, your next step is very clear. You need to cut your losses and **move on to your next job**. You need to be careful and make sure that you leave your new job carefully so that it doesn't look like you are running away from it.

None of us is perfect – we all have the ability to make the wrong decision at some point in time. What can make us a great CIO is the ability to **be aware that we've made a poor decision** and then the ability to react and make the right decision.

Chapter 9

Why Is The CIO Position Reporting Structure Broken?

Chapter 9: Why Is The CIO Position Reporting Structure Broken?

Don't look now, but there's something wrong in the world of CIOs. The CIOs that I'm working with are being asked to do more and more for their companies. It would be fair to say that IT has become an indispensable part of the companies that these CIOs work for. Then can you tell me why at some companies CIOs **don't report directly into the CEO?**

The Bad News

In a recent survey of firms, less than half of the firms that responded said that the CIO reported directly to the CEO. This means that even as IT becomes more and more important to the economic well-being of a firm, the person who has been tasked to implement the firm's IT strategy is **being prevented** from participating in the planning of the company's overall strategy.

What does this actually mean? In a nutshell, it means that a critical line of communication is longer and **more apt to break** than it needs to be. Considering all of the challenges that modern firms face, the CIO needs to be at the right hand of the CEO when ways to move the company forward are being discussed.

A good example of what can possibly happen if the CIO does not report directly to the CEO happed at Sony. Their Playstation network was hacked and confidential customer information was taken by parties unknown. As big and as sophisticated a company as Sony is, their CIO reports in to the Chief Transformation Officer who in turn reports in to the CEO. **Talk about a broken pipe!**

A Ray Of Hope?

The solution to this problem is clear: the position of CIO needs to **report directly into the CEO**. The challenge is finding out how to convince those 50% of firms that don't have this structure to make the changes that will be needed in order to make it happen.

The big question is what will motivate these firms to make this kind of change? As with all things in business, the reason for making a change needs to be **based on the company's bottom line**.

In the case of the CIO, it's the IT department activities that don't have anything to do with keeping the lights on that will provide **a compelling story** for having the CIO report directly to the CEO. Tasks such as mining the customer and sales data that the company has collected in order to gleam new customer needs and buying patterns are things that the CEO needs to both lead and respond to. The only way that this can happen is if the CEO and the CIO are directly talking.

Additionally, as the specter of digital break-ins becomes ever more possible, the CIO needs to be working with the CEO in order to determine what data needs to be stored, how long it needs to be stored, and when collected information can be disposed of. Only by agreeing on a company-wide policy and then implementing it can firms start to deal with creating an **effective defense** against being hacked.

What All Of This Means For You

All too often companies give **lip service** to the importance of IT to their overall success while at the same time relegating their CIOs to report to someone who is not the CEO. This contradiction clearly shows that something is broken at the top of many companies.

Recent surveys have revealed that CIOs reported directly to the CEO at less than half and maybe even fewer of the companies surveyed. What this means is simply that the CIO is not being heard where he or she needs to be heard: at the top of the company. As security threats grow and the value of business data becomes more and more important, this kind of organizational structure **cannot be permitted to remain in place**.

The change that needs to occur is that CIOs need to **report directly the company's CEO**. It's only by setting up this kind of reporting structure that the types of conversations that need to occur around data retention, infrastructure security, etc. will happen. Considering what the rest of the company is asking the CIO to accomplish, it sure seems as though inviting them to the big table is something that has to happen sooner rather than later.

Chapter 10

One Industry Finally Understands The Importance Of A CIO

Chapter 10: One Industry Finally Understands The Importance Of A CIO

'Tis the time of year that my CIO customers are starting to get itchy to **try new things**. The kids are out of school and greener pastures beckon. They keep asking me where they should be looking for their next CIO job. Is there any industry that will truly appreciate the value that a skilled CIO can bring to the job? It turns out that the answer is yes and right now I'm recommending one industry in particular: energy companies.

Why Energy Companies Love Their CIOs

In order for a CIO to be fully appreciated by their company, the company has to have **a real need for their services**. At this point in time, energy companies fit that bill – they are facing significant IT challenges.

The first thing that CIOs need to realize when they start to consider working for an energy company is just exactly **what an energy company does**. Yes, generating electricity is a big part of the company's job. However, there is a lot more going on.

Energy companies buy and sell energy and energy futures. They spend a great deal of time and effort planning how they will generate energy in the future. All of these tasks **require a lot of data**. Only now are energy companies starting to deal with just exactly how they are going to both store and access the large amounts of digital data that they need to more accurately perform their jobs.

Since energy companies are performing tasks that other firms are also doing, **benchmarking is a very valuable activity**. The CIO is needed in order to implement ways of performing ongoing benchmarking analysis with multiple other firms.

Finally, we are entering a new era of the **smart energy gird**. This means that sophisticated two-way meters are being installed in homes and businesses. The amount of real-time data that energy companies are going to have to process is getting ready to skyrocket. The CIO is going to be needed in order to create solutions for dealing with these new challenges.

Why Working For An Energy Company Is A Good Choice For CIOs

So now let's get down to the nitty-gritty: why am I telling my CIO clients to **look into CIO jobs in the energy industry?** The reasons are actually pretty simple. It all starts with the fact that the energy companies get it – information has become the ultimate competitive advantage and the CIO holds the key to providing the company with the information that they need.

In the world of energy companies **IT really matters**. Instead of being told what has been decided and asked to implement it, the IT department is being invited to the strategy table and their inputs are shaping what the company decides to do.

A recent study of energy company organizations revealed that 20% of CIOs in this industry **report directly to the CEO**. Additionally, 5% – 10% of the other firms are moving their CIOs up the organizational chart each year. Although the numbers aren't wonderful, they are a lot better than in other industries.

Finally, the Stuxnet virus that attacked the Iranian nuclear industry was **a wake-up call for energy companies everywhere**: it could happen to them. They are now all turning to their CIOs in order to be told what they need to do in order to keep their IT systems safe and their ability to generate energy on-line.

What All Of This Means For You

The CIOs that I spend my time helping all too often feel overlooked and underappreciated. When they finally get fed up with the CIO job that they have, they ask me **where they should go to look for their next CIO job**. I tell them that the energy companies are the ones who currently appreciate what a good CIO can do.

The reason that energy companies love their CIOs is because they have **specific needs that only the CIO can help them with**. These needs include securely storing and efficiently processing the mountains of data that are needed in order to determine how much it costs them to generate a kilowatt of energy. The arrival of the smart grid and smart meters has caused the data that an energy company has to process to skyrocket. Finally, security has become a constant topic of conversation as the importance of the national power grid has only recently started to be understood.

CIOs are people too. Just like everyone else they desperately **want their work to be appreciated**. This means that they need to work for a company that has real IT needs and will support them as they solve those needs. It may not be the case forever, but for now energy companies are a great place for CIOs to go looking for their next job!

Chapter 11

Do You Have Enough Personal Energy To Be CIO?

Chapter 11: Do You Have Enough Personal Energy To Be CIO?

So what's it going to take **to make you a successful CIO?** Is it going to be your understanding of a wide variety of the IT sector's emerging technologies? Is it your ability to understand where the company stands in the marketplace and where it wants to go? Or is it your business skills that allow you to seamlessly network with the rest of the company in order to lead the IT department?

Turns out that these are all good to have; however, what it's going to take to get you to the finish line is something much more valuable: personal energy.

Why You Are Doing A Poor Job Of Being CIO

How would you be able to tell if you were **doing a poor job of being CIO?** I guess one way would be to determine that you were not getting things done – more and more tasks were just sitting around waiting for you to get to them. Is this happening? Maybe we should take a look at your email inbox – is it getting rather full?

So what's going on here? You've probably read that "Getting Things Done" book, you've studied the 7 habits of effective people, how much more time can you spend managing your time? Tony Schwartz has looked into what is going on here and he believes that we are all experiencing what he calls a **"personal energy crisis"**.

Look, for years and years we have all been finding ways to **do more in a fixed amount of time** – thank you smart phones and laptops. However, we've just about used up all of our available time no matter how hard we try to free up more time to do stuff. We are out of time. Going forward it's not going to be so much about finding more time to get things done, rather it's all going to be about finding the personal energy to get things done.

How To Find Your Personal Power

The concept of having enough personal power to get the important work done seems straightforward enough. But how does one actually go about doing this? Here's what we are all missing: we are human beings and that means that at a biological level we are programmed to work for a while and then to **take a rest**. The definition of information technology focuses on the software and systems that we use to accomplish tasks – we are not those machines. We are not computers sitting in some data center somewhere that can be plugged in and run for months or years without stopping.

Ooops, did I say rest? Doesn't that **go against** just about everything that you are currently doing? Didn't you get to the position of CIO by working harder than everyone else? Getting in early, staying late, working weekends is what it takes to succeed, right?

Bad / Good news – turns out that we've got it all wrong. Because we are human beings, we do need rest. But the good thing about rest is that after we get some, we have the ability to do more work than before. Studies of pilots have shown this to be true: a short half-hour nap boosted their reaction times by 16% while pilots who didn't nap had their reaction times drop by 34%. I suspect that most of us are in the 34% crowd.

A sleep researcher named Nathaniel Kleitman came up with the concept of the **"basic rest activity cycle"**. What this means is that during the day we all cycle through a 90-minute cycle where we go from high alertness to low alertness. Clearly your body wants you to stop and take a break every 90 minutes or so.

To become a more effective CIO you need to make some changes in how you run your day. You need to schedule your work so that you are running at a higher focus for a shorter period of time. After this period is over, you need to **take the time to rest and allow your body to renew itself**. By doing this you will find that you really can get more work done in less time!

What All Of This Means For You

In order to be an effective CIO you are going to have to be able to get an awful lot of work done. The question that should be smacking you in the face right about now is just exactly **how are you going to get all of that work done?** It turns out that time management is only going to get you so far. You are eventually going to run out of time.

The importance of information technology means that you need to become a strong leader, not one that runs out of steam. You are going to have to switch from managing your time to **managing your personal energy**. We humans are designed to work in 90 minute cycles. What this means that is that we'll go from being very alert to being not so alert every hour and a half. Understanding that you have this cycle and designing your work schedule around it will be the key to becoming and remaining effective.

You can become the CIO that everyone turns to because they know that you can get it done. However, the only way that you're going to be able to do this is to make sure that **your personal energy** is up to powering you through day after day of charting your company's technological future. Start living your work days 90 minutes at a time and you'll be the CIO that everyone looks up to.

Chapter 12

Great CIOs Aren't Afraid To Stumble On The Way To The Top

Chapter 12: Great CIOs Aren't Afraid To Stumble On The Way To The Top

A quick question for you: **are you afraid to fail?** Would you be willing to take on responsibility for an IT department that might not be a success? I'm willing to bet that a lot of us would say "no" – CIOs who are perfect are rewarded while CIOs who fail are kicked to the curb. However, I'm going to tell you that you're wrong – get ready to fail if you want to succeed.

How To Kill Your CIO Career

In your job right now, if you fail then that end-of-year review would be a tough one to sit through, right? Let's face it, failure is not something that is rewarded in our workplace and in fact it's something that **we all actively avoid** if we possibly can.

However, maybe we're just setting ourselves up for a much bigger career disaster. Can we all admit that **the world as we know it is changing**? Can you remember watching old-time movies where the hero would get a job at a company and then spend his or her entire career working there? We all know that those days are long gone.

Something else is changing also: our jobs. The job that you had when you started working may already be gone. The CIO one that you're doing right now probably won't exist in what, 2, maybe 3 years from now. This all means that **you are going to have to change** and change involves risk and along with risk comes the very real possibility that you are going to fail.

How To Become A Success By Failing

Well, that failing stuff doesn't sound like it's going to be any fun. But wait, **has anyone else ever failed?** Turns out that yes, in fact most successful people can look at their past and point to failures that helped them to get to where they are now.

The poster child for this kind of "good failure" would be Howard Schultz – the guy who founded **the Starbucks chain of coffee shops**. We all know and love the Starbucks store today, but when Howard first started it he really blew it. There were no chairs, he played lots of opera music, and his menu was in Italian. Clearly he quickly realized that he had failed, adjusted, and went on to become a big success.

You can do the same. You need to **learn to make lots of small bets**. Some of these bets will pay off, and some won't. It's through what you learn from the failures that you'll be able to make tiny changes to your approach and try, try again.

If we keep doing things the same way that we've always been doing them, then we will eventually stagnate and then **we'll go into decline**. However, if you have the courage to start to fail and to learn from those failures, then the future contains limitless possibilities for both you and your career.

What All Of This Means For You

CIOs who are afraid to fail **will never become a true success**. Oh sure, they may do ok for a few years, but when things get really rough, they'll wash out.

If you are willing to adjust how you view failure, **your career can take off**. If you can start to look at failures as being simply being learning experiences that are not be feared, but they are to be used to become a better CIO then you'll be able to grow and become better at what you do.

No, you can't be an idiot about this and do silly things that cause your IT department to fail, but if you try your hardest and your department still fails than **you will have learned what doesn't work**. The big deal is that it takes courage for you to be able to do this.

CIOs who are a success have to had failures in their past. It's from the forge of failure that the steel of success is formed. Learn how to make small bets so that **you can learn what works** and what doesn't. Do this well and you'll become a successful CIO.

It's from the forge of failure that the steel of success is formed.

Hard Work Does Not Guarantee Success, But Success Does Not Happen Without Hard Work.

- Dr. Jim Anderson

Create IT Departments That Are Productive And A Valuable Asset To The Rest Of The Company !

Dr. Jim Anderson is available to provide training and coaching on the topics that are the most important to people who have to manage IT departments: how can I build a productive IT department (and keep it together) while at the same time providing the rest of the company with the IT services that they need?

Dr. Anderson believes that in order to both learn and remember what he says, speakers need to laugh. Each one of his speeches is full of fun and humor so that what he says "sticks" with everyone.

Dr. Anderson's CIO Skills Training Includes:

1. How to identify and attract the right type of IT workers to your IT department.
2. How to build relationships with the company's senior management in order to get the support that you need?
3. How to stay on top of changing technology and security issues so that you never get surprised?

Dr. Jim Anderson works with over 100 customers per year. To invite Dr. Anderson to work with you, contact him at:

Phone: 813-418-6970 or
Email: jim@BlueElephantConsulting.com

Speaking Negotiating Managing Marketing

12

Photo Credits:

Chapter 6 - Marc Moss

https://www.flickr.com/photos/lovenotfear/

Chapter 7 – click

http://d3graphix.yolasite.com

Chapter 8 – wallyir

https://morguefile.com/p/676238

Chapter 9 - Pulpolux !!!

http://www.flickr.com/photos/pulpolux/3932292651/sizes/l/in/photostream/

Chapter 10 - earl53

https://morguefile.com/p/101599

Chapter 11 - Xavier Vergés

https://www.flickr.com/photos/xverges/

Chapter 12 - jon Jordan

https://www.flickr.com/photos/jontintinjordan/

Other Books By The Author

Product Management

- Manage Your Customers, Manage Your Product: Techniques For Product Managers To Better Understand What Their Customers Really Want

- How Product Managers Can Sell More Of Their Product: Tips & Techniques For Product Managers To Better Understand How To Sell Their Product

- How Product Managers Can Sell More Of Their Product: Tips & Techniques For Product Managers To Better Understand How To Sell Their Product

- How To Create A Successful Product That Customers Will Want: Techniques For Product Managers To Boost Product Sales And Increase Customer Satisfaction

- What Product Managers Need To Know About World-Class Product Development: How Product Managers Can Create Successful Products

- How Product Managers Can Learn To Understand Their Customers: Techniques For Product Managers To Better Understand What Their Customers Really Want

- Product Management Secrets: Techniques For Product Managers To Boost Product Sales And Increase Customer Satisfaction

- Product Development Lessons For Product Managers: How Product Managers Can Create Successful Products

- Customer Lessons For Product Managers: Techniques For Product Managers To Better Understand What Their Customers Really Want

- Product Failure Lessons For Product Managers: Examples Of Products That Have Failed For Product Managers To Learn From

- Communication Skills For Product Managers: The Communication Skills That Product Managers Need To Know How To Use In Order To Have A Successful Product

- How To Have A Successful Product Manager Career: The Things That You Need To Be Doing TODAY In Order To Have A Successful Product Manager Career

- Product Manager Product Success: How to keep your product on track and make it become a success

Public Speaking

- How To Get Ready To Give The Perfect Speech: What Tools To Use To Create Your Next Speech So That Your Message Will Be Remembered Forever!

- Creating Speeches That Work: How To Create A Speech That Will Make Your Message Be Remembered Forever!

- How To Organize A Speech In Order To Make Your Point: How to put together a speech that will capture and hold your audience's attention

- Changing How You Speak To Overcome Your Fear Of Speaking: Change techniques that will transform a speech into a memorable event

- Delivering Excellence: How To Give Presentations That Make A Difference: Presentation techniques that will transform a speech into a memorable event

- Tools Speakers Need In Order To Give The Perfect Speech: What tools to use to create your next speech so that your message will be remembered forever!

- How To Create A Speech That Will Be Remembered

- Secrets To Organizing A Speech For Maximum Impact: How to put together a speech that will capture and hold your audience's attention

- How To Become A Better Speaker By Changing How You Speak: Change techniques that will transform a speech into a memorable event

- How To Give A Great Presentation: Presentation techniques that will transform a speech into a memorable event

- How To Rehearse In Order To Give The Perfect Speech: How to effectively rehearse your next speech to that your message be remembered forever!

- Secrets To Creating The Perfect Speech: How to create a speech that will make your message be remembered forever!

- Secrets To Organizing The Perfect Speech: How to organize the best speech of your life!

- Secrets To Planning The Perfect Speech: How to plan to give the best speech of your life

- How To Show What You Mean During A Presentation: How to use visual techniques to transform a speech into a memorable event

CIO Skills

- How CIOs Can Bring Business And IT Together: How CIOs Can Use Their Technical Skills To Help Their Company Solve Real-World Business Problems

- New IT Technology Issues Facing CIOs: How CIOs Can Stay On Top Of The Changes In The Technology That Powers The Company

- Keeping The Barbarians Out: How CIOs Can Secure Their Department and Company: Tips And Techniques For CIOs To Use In Order To Secure Both Their IT Department And Their Company

- What CIOs Need To Know In Order To Successfully Manage An IT Department: Decision Making Skills That Every CIO Needs To Have In Order To Be Able To Make The Right Choices

- Becoming A Powerful And Effective Leader: Tips And Techniques That IT Managers Can Use In Order To Develop Leadership Skills

- CIO Secrets For Growing Innovation: Tips And Techniques For CIOs To Use In Order To Make Innovation Happen In Their IT Department

- Your Success As A CIO Depends On How Well You Communicate: Tips And Techniques For CIOs To Use In Order To Become Better Communicators

- What CIOs Need To Know About Working With Partners: Techniques For CIOs To Use In Order To Be Able To Successfully Work With Partners

- Critical CIO Management Skills: Decision Making Skills That Every CIO Needs To Have In Order To Be Able To Make The Right Choices

- How CIOs Can Make Innovation Happen: Tips And Techniques For CIOs To Use In Order To Make Innovation Happen In Their IT Department

- CIO Communication Skills Secrets: Tips And Techniques For CIOs To Use In Order To Become Better Communicators

- Managing Your CIO Career: Steps That CIOs Have To Take In Order To Have A Long And Successful Career

- CIO Business Skills: How CIOs can work effectively with the rest of the company!

IT Manager Skills

- How IT Managers Can Use New Technology To Meet Today's IT Challenges: Technologies That IT Managers Can Use In Order to Make Their Teams More Productive

- How To Build High Performance IT Teams: Tips And Techniques That IT Managers Can Use In Order

To Develop Productive Teams

- Save Yourself, Save Your Job – How To Manage Your IT Career: Secrets That IT Managers Can Use In Order To Have A Successful Career

- Growing Your CIO Career: How CIOs Can Work With The Entire Company In Order To Be Successful

- How IT Managers Can Make Innovation Happen: Tips And Techniques For IT Managers To Use In Order To Make Innovation Happen In Their Teams

- Staffing Skills IT Managers Must Have: Tips And Techniques That IT Managers Can Use In Order To Correctly Staff Their Teams

- Secrets Of Effective Leadership For IT Managers: Tips And Techniques That IT Managers Can Use In Order To Develop Leadership Skills

- IT Manager Career Secrets: Tips And Techniques That IT Managers Can Use In Order To Have A Successful Career

- IT Manager Budgeting Skills: How IT Managers Can Request, Manage, Use, And Track Their Funding

- Secrets Of Managing Budgets: What IT Managers Need To Know In Order To Understand How Their Company Uses Money

Negotiating

- The Art Of Packaging A Negotiation: How To Develop The Skill Of Assembling Potential Trades In Order To Get The Best Possible Outcome

- Getting What You Want In A Negotiation By Learning How To Signal: How To Develop The Skill Of Effective Signaling In A Negotiation In Order To Get The Best Possible Outcome

- Exploring How To Get The Deal That You Want In A Negotiation: How To Develop The Skill Of Exploring What Is Possible In A Negotiation In Order To Reach The Best Possible Deal

- Use The Power Of Arguing To Win Your Next Negotiation: How To Develop The Skill Of Effective Arguing In A Negotiation In Order To Get The Best Possible Outcome

- Learn How To Signal In Your Next Negotiation: How To Develop The Skill Of Effective Signaling In A Negotiation In Order To Get The Best Possible Outcome

- Learn The Skill Of Exploring In A Negotiation: How To Develop The Skill Of Exploring What Is Possible In A Negotiation In Order To Reach The Best Possible Deal

- Learn How To Argue In Your Next Negotiation: How To Develop The Skill Of Effective Arguing In A Negotiation In Order To Get The Best Possible Outcome|

- How To Open Your Next Negotiation: How To Start A Negotiation In Order To Get The Best Possible Outcome

- Preparing For Your Next Negotiation: What You Need To Do BEFORE A Negotiation Starts In Order To Get The Best Possible Deal

- Learn How To Package Trades In Your Next Negotiation

- All Good Things Come To An End: How To Close A Negotiation - How To Develop The Skill Of Closing In Order To Get The Best Possible Outcome From A Negotiation

- Take No Prisoners In Your Next Negotiation: How To Start A Negotiation In Order To Get The Best Possible Outcome

Miscellaneous

- How To Heal A Broken Leg – Fast!: Understanding how to deal with a broken leg in order to start walking again quickly

- How Software Defined Networking (SDN) Is Going To Change Your World Forever: The Revolution In Network Design And How It Affects You

- The Power Of Virtualization: How It Affects Memory, Servers, and Storage: The Revolution In Creating Virtual Devices And How It Affects You

- The Internet-Enabled Successful School District Superintendent: How To Use The Internet To Boost Parental Involvement In Your Schools

- Power Distribution Unit (PDU) Secrets: What Everyone Who Works In A Data Center Needs To Know!

- Making The Jump: How To Land Your Dream Job When You Get Out Of College!

- How To Use The Internet To Create Successful Students And Involved Parents

How CIOs Can Work With The Entire Company In Order To Be Successful

This book has been written with one goal in mind – to show you how you can successfully grow your CIO career. It's not easy being a CIO so we're going to show you what you need to be doing in order to make your career a success!

Let's Make Your CIO Career A Success!

What You'll Find Inside:

- **CIO'S WITH NO TIME FIND AN ALTERNATIVE TO AN MBA**

- **THE "R" WORD AND WHAT IT MEANS TO CIOS**

- **WHY IS THE CIO POSITION REPORTING STRUCTURE BROKEN?**

- **DO YOU HAVE ENOUGH PERSONAL ENERGY TO BE CIO?**

Dr. Jim Anderson brings his 25 years of real-world experience to this book. He's been a senior IT executive at some of the world's largest firms. He's going to show you what you need to do (and not do!) in order to make your CIO career a success!

www.ingramcontent.com/pod-product-compliance
Lightning Source LLC
Chambersburg PA
CBHW071759170526
45167CB00003B/1097

9 781543 248395